Will Macdonald

HOW TO BE A
PUB GENIUS

Will Macdonald

HOW TO BE A
PUB GENIUS

Fifty brilliant tricks guaranteed to wow babes and win beer

Virgin

For CLT
(that's just won me another pint)

Many thanks to – Rod Green for his eternal help and Scottishness,
Nathan for throaty northern keenness and the keys, Mr P Gascoigne
for 'Follow My Leader', ah! D Baker (he'll tell us what to do), Joely,
Keef & Son, Grave, Suzi, Barty, Ray, Coisty, the BNC bar, the KA,
The Duke's Head, Whitley, Johnny the photoman, Burgs for the early
nurturing through pubs, my brother Jonny for the training if not the
hair, all Macdonalds and Sullivans, and generally everyone who's
ever been to the pub. And especially to the 'wacky ginger guy'
(said with an American accent) who puts me off doing these tricks
on *TFI Friday* by grabbing my crotch under the desk.

Anyone fancy a pint?

First published in 1998 by
Virgin Publishing Ltd
Thames Wharf Studios
Rainville Road
London W6 9HT

Text copyright © Will Macdonald 1998

All photographs © RSA Photography

The right of Will Macdonald to be identified as the author of this
work has been asserted by him in accordance with the Copyright,
Designs and Patents Act 1988.

A catalogue record for this book is available from the British Library.

ISBN 0 7535 0310 7

Designed by Blackjacks, London

Printed by The Bath Press, Bath

CONTENTS

FOREWORD

When American inventor Thomas Alva Edison wrote 'Genius is 1 per cent inspiration, 99 per cent perspiration,' what he actually meant was 'Genius is 1 per cent inspiration, 99 per cent pub.'

You see, it's all very well being Albert Einstein and revolutionising modern science theory, but when was the last time his knowledge of relativity won him a pint? Yes, yes, Mr Marconi, radio is very clever, but you can't get lager with high-frequency alternating currents. And Leonardo da Vinci, James Joyce and Socrates may be sitting round a small, beer-stained circular table at the Old Slug and Combine Harvester, but are they having any fun?

No.

It's all very well being a genius in astrophysics or Dadaism, but it's not going to impress everyone, is it? You want to be a genius in the one place everyone cares about – the battle cruiser, the drinkery, the filling station, the rubbidy, the leeky store, the jinny, the slygrog shop, the juice house. You wanna be a pub genius.

No more sitting all alone at the end of the bar staring at a copy of last week's *Sun* for you. Imagine yourself surrounded by beautiful ladies all throwing their heads back in uncontrollable laughter, and a bunch of hunky guys all open-mouthed in astonishment as they reach for their wallets to buy you yet another drink. What a world to live in.

Well, if you follow the instructions laid out in this book, you could become that crowd-pulling hero. A local hero, if you like. Don't get me wrong. You don't have to be an alcoholic to be a pub genius. You can sit at home with your friends performing these tricks whilst having a post-pottery-class coffee. But you may find the booze-induced lower-expectation atmosphere of the pub better – and remember, Genius is an anagram of Use Gin.

What is a Pub Genius?

The Pub Genius(™) is the person who can keep the entertainment going long after the chat about football, Joey from *Friends* and that miserable-bloke-in-the-corner-who-never-lets-you-take-the-spare-chair-next-to-him-because-he-says-his-friend-is-coming-but-no-one-has-turned-up-in-the-last-four-years has dried up – and by using a few props from around the pub can win beer and that most valuable of currencies in the boozer – laughter.

The tricks in this book are ones that I have picked up from years of hardened experiences in the saloon bars and snugs of Great Britain*. I've been the victim of many of them myself, and it's much more enjoyable dishing this stuff out than being on the receiving end. I've also learnt it's important to try them out first before you do them, otherwise you end up with lager in your lap and egg on your face.

For most of the tricks, you don't need prestidigitational skills (although the ability to say that after an evening in the pub is a skill in itself) – so none of this sleight-of-hand nonsense is needed – it's more about lateral thinking (and lateral drinking) and a small bit of sly skulduggery.

The beauty of many of these tricks is that you can slip them into an evening (or afternoon (or morning)) like they've come off the top of your head. See a salt cellar out of the corner of your eye and you know you can fish an ice cube out of a gin and tonic with a piece of cotton. As someone pulls out a cigarette, tell them you can tie a knot in it. Drink a pint without touching it and make an orange dance.

Like joke-telling (an art form in which I have no skill whatsoever. Skeleton walks into a pub and asks for a pint of lager and a mop. See?), the secret is often more in the telling than the quality of the material. If you can make people believe that a challenge is not possible, then the simple solution you show them will get a bigger reaction and a larger 'DOH!' And it's about timing – choose the moments to do tricks and you'll be really cool – especially if the trick involves five bricks and a microwave.

The contents of this book can be used to win beer, wine, or Malibu and pineapple, to woo that someone special, or maybe even to bring world leaders closer together – after all, they have glasses, water, matches and probably beer at those G7 conferences, and Boris Yeltsin is always after another free drink.

Anyway, whatever you use these tricks for, have fun – even if they go wrong. God knows they've gone wrong enough times for me.

* *These tricks can be performed outside the UK, but always check beer-glass sizes and regional sense of humour.*

Suck on

What you need for this trick are seven pound coins – always the tricky bit – an empty ashtray, a box of matches and some beer in a half-pint glass.

Pile the coins in the centre of the ashtray and pour in the beer to create a little £1 island.

Now, the question is, how do you get the beer back into the glass without touching the ashtray or disturbing the coins?

this

1 Strike a match and balance it on top of the coins with the burning end hanging over the edge of the £1 island so that it will continue to burn.

2 Place the upturned beer glass over the island. As the match burns and uses up the air inside the glass, the beer will be drawn up out of the ashtray.

3 The beer is now back in the glass and you haven't touched the ashtray at all.

Practise this a few times so that you are able to judge roughly how much beer you need to use. Best use your own beer, too, because no one's going to want it back after it's been poured into an ashtray and flavoured with smoke from a burning match. Turning it back the right way up can also be a bit messy . . .

The Penny's

Although it does, naturally, look impossible when you set it up, this is quite an easy trick to do. It's also the first trick that went wrong on TFI Friday!

For The Penny's Dropped, you require a penny (a 2p coin is actually best), a cigarette (you don't need to smoke to do this trick – although, kids, smoking's great*), a beer mat and a wine glass.

Place the beer mat flat on the wine glass, then stand the cigarette on it. Finally balance the coin on top of the cigarette. You'll need a steady hand, but it's not too difficult with a bit of practice and providing that you haven't had too many drinks beforehand. (One drink will steady your hand, two will steady your head, five will shteady you shand. And what are you looking at, pal?)

Although it's a feat in itself, the balancing act is not the trick. What you do next is ask your audience how you get the coin into the glass without touching any of the objects. It's worth betting a pint on this one.

Dropped

1 So how is it done? Simple. You just blow upward under the edge of the beer mat. The mat will blow away, taking the cigarette with it.

2 The coin then drops straight into the glass.

*No it's not

Get Knotted

How do you tie a cigarette in a knot without breaking it? Can't be done? Of course it can, and here's how.

What you will need is a cigarette, obviously, and the cellophane wrapping from a pack of cigarettes. Take the cigarette from a friend and promise you'll give it back in one piece – you know, like a magician does.

1 Open out the cellophane and lay it flat on the table, then place the cigarette on the celliphane so there is an overlap on either side of it. Start rolling it inside the cellophane, wrapping it as tightly as you can, just like you're rolling a 'Woodbine'. Make sure the cellophane is nice and tight without any folds or creases in it.

2 Twist the ends to stop it unwrapping and flatten out the cellophane beyond the twist to make something that looks like a thin Christmas cracker.

3 Holding on to the flattened ends of cellophane, tie them into a knot. The cigarette inside will then knot as well.

4 If the cellophane is tight enough, the cigarette paper shouldn't burst as you tie the knot.

5 Untie the knot and unwrap the cigarette. It might look a little worse for wear, but it should still be whole!

Olive ...?er

For this trick you need an olive, a brandy glass, two wine glasses, a drinking straw and a half-pint glass.

Arrange the glasses as shown, with the straw forming a hurdle supported by the wine glasses. Bet a friend a pint they can't get the olive over the hurdle and into the half-pint glass without touching, flicking, scooping, pinging or eating the olive.

Can't be done? I think you'll find it can!

1. Place the upturned brandy glass over the olive and start to whirl it round, rotating the glass in a furious clockwise circular motion. The olive will spin round and rise up inside the brandy glass.

Twist

CAUTION:
You must keep the brandy glass level as you carry the olive over the hurdle. If you tilt it, the olive will fly out at great speed and, although not lethal to whomever ll hits, if it hurtles across to the next table and catches that 6ft 4in Millwall supporter on the back of the head, your health could suffer as a result.

2 Keep the manic spinning going and lift the glass off the table. As long as you keep up the circular motion, the olive will continue to spin round inside the brandy glass. Don't pause for a break or it'll fall out.

3 Still spinning, carry the olive over the hurdle, lower the brandy glass down over the half-pint glass and stop spinning. The olive will drop into the half-pint glass.

Jumper

This is an excellent trick for winning a swift half of beer.

You'll need one of your mates (if you have any left after you've been trying out all these tricks), a jumper and half a pint of beer – preferably bought by your mate.

You cover the half-pint with the jumper and bet your mate that you can drink the beer without wetting, damaging or even touching the jumper. No one in their right mind will believe you can do it, but the beer's as good as yours.

Here's how it's done.

Jehossefat

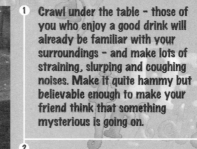

1 Crawl under the table – those of you who enjoy a good drink will already be familiar with your surroundings – and make lots of straining, slurping and coughing noises. Make it quite hammy but believable enough to make your friend think that something mysterious is going on.

2 Crawl out again and take your seat. Point to the jumper with a flourish and tell your mate to 'take it away!' as though the trick is complete. When he's taken it away, the beer, of course, is still there.

3 Pick up the beer and drink it. Well, you haven't touched the jumper, have you? Grrr!

NOTE: If it's summer and you're not wearing that Pringle tank top, then you can put the beer under a hat. Failing that a small box. Failing that . . . oh, you decide . . .

Can Be Done

How do you balance an ordinary can of soft drink on its edge without damaging the can or using any other props? (I know that reverting to non-alcohol is hard, but having said that it might work with a can of lager.)

Try balancing the pristine can on its rim to show everyone how impossible this trick is. People might expect you to slam it into the table to flatten an edge but, remember, you're not allowed to damage the can.

So how's it done? Simple!

1 Open the can and drink about one third of the contents. Hold back your urge to drink it all.

2 Carefully set the can at an angle. The drink inside will now have room to move around and settle, helping to balance the can.

3 With a little patience and concentration, you will be able to balance the can on its rim!

A (Sherry) ?

This trick is a little complicated but looks great if you can do it without choking or drowning in sherry.

What you need is a glass of sherry, so it's a good one to do if you have the vicar round, and an empty brandy glass.

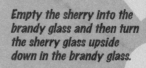

Empty the sherry into the brandy glass and then turn the sherry glass upside down in the brandy glass.

The question is, how do you drink the sherry out of the sherry glass without handling the sherry glass?

Don't try this if your false teeth are a bit loose.

Trifle Tricky

1 Clasp the rim of the sherry glass gently between your teeth. You have to reach over and take the side farthest away from you in your mouth.

2 Lift the sherry glass clear of the brandy glass.

3 Tilt your head back so that the sherry glass is level and the right way up.

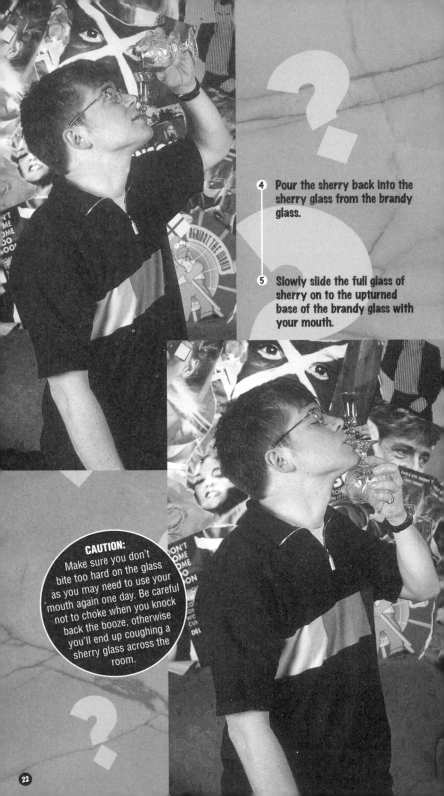

4 Pour the sherry back into the sherry glass from the brandy glass.

5 Slowly slide the full glass of sherry on to the upturned base of the brandy glass with your mouth.

CAUTION:
Make sure you don't bite too hard on the glass as you may need to use your mouth again one day. Be careful not to choke when you knock back the booze, otherwise you'll end up coughing a sherry glass across the room.

6 Once you have the sherry safely balanced on the upturned brandy glass . . .

7 . . . take the entire sherry glass in your mouth and knock it back in a oner!

8 Remove sherry glass from gob and offer the vicar another drink.

NOTE: When I did this on *TFI Friday*, unbeknownst to me Keef substituted Bacardi Spice for the sherry, which explained the puce colour I went afterwards. Thanks, Keef.

The Big

For this elaborate and hilarious stunt you will need four pints of lager. Borrow them off friends. You'll also need a tray from the bar, the sleeves from four matchboxes and four hardboiled eggs. You might be able to get the eggs from your landlady; if not, take four from that jar of pickled eggs behind the bar which hasn't been opened since the war. The last thing you need is the broom that has doubtless been used countless times to sweep you out the door at closing time.

Place the tray on top of the pints of lager and then balance the four eggs on top of the matchbox sleeves, arranging them on the tray directly above the pints of lager. You will have to squeeze the matchbox sleeves slightly to make them a little rounder in order for the eggs to sit comfortably on top.

So much for the setup, but what's the amazing stunt? Well, the aim is to get the eggs into the pints of lager without touching the beer glasses, the matchboxes or the eggs – and using only the broom. Give the watching multitudes a load of old flannel to make them think the broom might be used for sweeping or something.

Brush Off

1

Climb up on the table and hold the broom a bit like a croquet mallet. What do you mean you've never played croquet? OK, just hold it as I'm doing in the photo.

CAUTION:
Be sure to plot the trajectory of the tray. Its flight across a crowded pub could dismay some people, especially the parents of the nine-year-old kid whose head you've just removed in the ensuing human/tray interface.

2

Swing the broom handle back and, with one short, sharp jab, knock the tray straight off the tops of the glasses. The matchboxes will be carried away with the tray and the eggs will drop into the glasses.

TIP:
Although you're looking for a short, sharp contact with the tray, try to follow through with the broom handle. This will help to ensure that the tray clears the glasses.

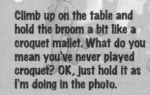

Flash the Ash

The challenge here is to let a whole cigarette, held horizontally, burn down to the filter without any of the ash falling off. You will be able to hold the cigarette perfectly naturally, even move it around, and all you need to do it is a paper clip.

You don't have to smoke to be able to do this trick: the cigarette will burn perfectly well without you sucking on it and the effect will be the same – total astonishment on the faces of anyone watching.

1 First straighten out the paper clip (something that anyone who works in an office probably spends most of their time doing, anyway), then measure it up against the cigarette and break off enough of the straightened clip so that you are left with a piece of wire slightly longer than the white part of the cigarette.

2 Next, gently push the wire up inside the cigarette. Make sure you don't burst the paper by shoving the end through the side of the cigarette. Part of the wire should enter the filter, leaving none of it visible.

3 Then, you light up and let it burn.

4 The ash will grow and grow as the cigarette burns down, but it won't fall off.

TIP:
You can either bet your mates that you can smoke a whole cigarette without the ash falling off and do the trick in front of them, having brought a paper clip with you, or you can insert the wire before you go down the pub and just watch their faces as you light up and let the ash get longer and longer.

Can I Have

All you need for this trick is two empty straight pint glasses. For reasons that will become obvious, you can't use handled glasses. Either get the glasses from your landlady, or buy two pints and drink them – it's up to you.

Stack one inside the other and lay them down at the edge of the table. Now – how do you separate them without touching them in any way or moving the table?

Can't be done? It can if you've got any breath left after making those pints disappear.

Your Glasses?

① Bend down and blow into the gap just inside the rim of the outside glass.

② The inside glass will shoot out. Catch it before it hits the floor!

Match That,

This trick involves a matchbox, two matches and a coin.

Set the trick up as shown. Stand one match up jammed vertically in the drawer of the matchbox. Place the coin on top of the matchbox and then balance the second match with its base on the coin and its head resting against the head of the other match.

Next you can bet your friends the coin – in this case a 2p, so it might be better to wager a round of drinks – that you can remove the coin from the top of the matchbox without touching the matches, knocking them over, or moving the box.

Can't be done? Well pay attention ...

① Take another match, obviously from some other matchbox, strike it and apply it to the heads of the two matches. The matchheads will flare up and weld themselves together.

Wise Guy

2 As they burn, the match resting on the coin will rise up.

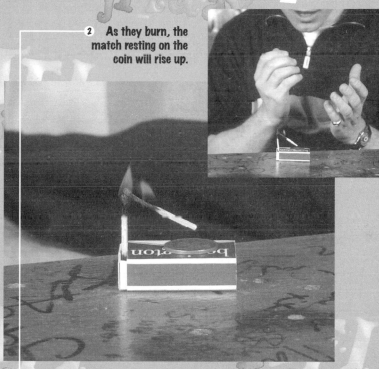

3 As if by magic (the Shopkeeper doesn't appear), the base of the match will clear the coin.

4 Once the match is out of the way, simply pick up the coin – and order your drink from whoever's buying the next round.

Trouble & Knife

Here's a seemingly impossible task. How do you balance the full wine glass on top of the knives so that it's above the three glasses – and at least six inches away from them.

Give in?

You're just not trying hard enough!

This is how it's done . . .

① Arrange the three empty glasses in a triangle and then 'weave' the blades of the three knives together in an over-and-under, interlocking pattern.

2 Balance the handles of the knives on the rims of the glasses, then carefully place the full wine glass in the centre.

3 Sit back and accept the applause!

Hi-Karate

You'll need a pint of lager – don't make it premium lager as this could be the last you'll see of it. You may never get to drink this pint. This trick is that risky. You'll also need a matchbox . . . and nerves of steel!

Balance the pint on top of the matchbox. The question is, how do you get the matchbox from under the pint without touching the pint?

Can't be done? On several occasions when I've tried it, like on TFI Friday, I'm sorry to say you'd have been right, but this trick can be done if you're brave, skilful and daring.

① Lay your hand flat on the table and concentrate on the matchbox.

2 Dramatically measure up for a rapid, sweeping, Kung-Fu style slice. You must be able to keep your hand flat on the table and . . .

3 . . . slash your hand under the glass, following straight through. You *should* knock the matchbox out from under the glass without it tipping over.

Take it on t

For this trick you will need an empty half-pint glass, a not-so-empty half-pint glass and a good set of teeth. Borrow someone else's if you don't want to risk your own.

Place the empty glass upside down on top of the glass with the beer in it. The object of the exercise is to drink the beer without handling either glass.

Can't be done? It can with the chin of a Pub Genius!

1 What you do is trap the top glass under your chin and lift it clear of the bottom glass.

e Chin

CAUTION:
For this stunt it is best to use a plastic glass - if that's not an oxymoron.

2 Next you lean forward, still clutching the top glass under your chin, and grasp the bottom glass with your teeth.

3 Then, you lean back and drink.

It does help if you've got a double or even a treble chin for this trick. Obviously I rely on skill alone.

The Brickie's Lift

You might not find five house bricks readily available in your local, unless they're renovating the gents or something, so these are props that you will have to bring with you. For goodness sake don't get caught 'borrowing' them from the building site next door. Remember, the brickie's probably in the pub with you.

So, you have five bricks. The challenge is to lift all five bricks off the table together using only one hand – and you're not allowed to slide them off the edge of the table or use any other kind of backsliding skulduggery. It's got to be a straight lift.

So how's it done?

❶ Place one brick on edge, then arrange two bricks on top, running across the first brick at either end.

2 The remaining two bricks go on top of the two cross-bricks in a third layer running in the same direction as the first brick.

3 Then you reach down through the gap and grasp the bottom brick.

4 You can now lift all five bricks, but not for very long unless you're Arnold Schwarzenegger. (And if you are, then welcome to the book, Arnie.)

The Final

Seven six-inch nails and a hammer? OK, you might not find them lying around on the bar, but you managed to get hold of five bricks for the last trick, didn't you? This trick forms a fine piece of modern sculpture which would be worth millions if it was displayed in the Tate, but could easily get you banned from your local.

The challenge is to balance six nails on top of just one nail so that none of the six is touching the table.

Can't be done? It can with a little ingenuity.

What you have to do is . . .

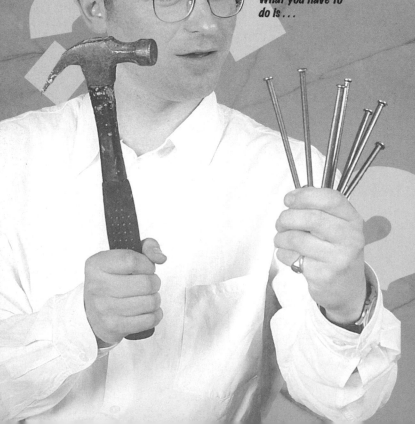

Nail

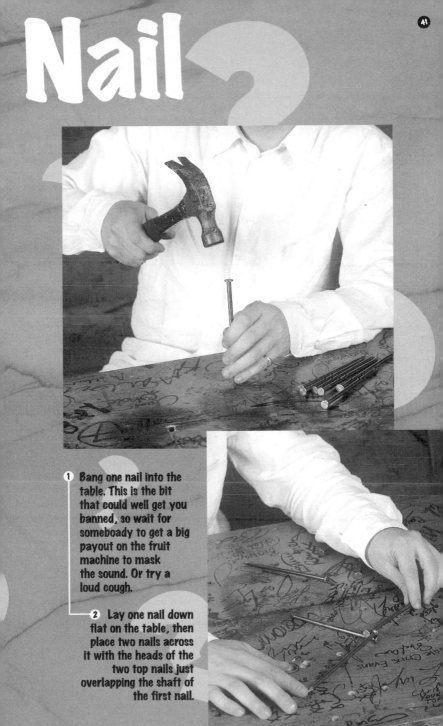

1. Bang one nail into the table. This is the bit that could well get you banned, so wait for someboady to get a big payout on the fruit machine to mask the sound. Or try a loud cough.

2. Lay one nail down flat on the table, then place two nails across it with the heads of the two top nails just overlapping the shaft of the first nail.

3 Arrange the next two nails in a similar fashion at the other end of the first nail.

4 The last nail then goes on top, lying in the same direction as the first nail and resting in the groove created by the heads of the others.

5 Now take hold of the first nail and you can lift the whole lot clear of the table. The arrangement of nails will form a kind of tent shape as you pick it up, with the top nail holding the others in place.

6 You can now balance your tent of nails on the head of the one you banged into the table.

There you have it – six nails balanced on top of just one, and, to make your Damien Hirst structure even more exciting, gently push the nail tent so that it rotates on top of the vertical nail. Wow!

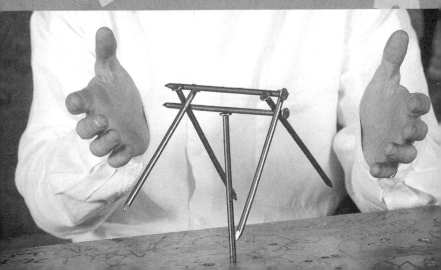

Gone Fishing

Here's a trick you can do if someone at your table has a drink with ice in it. They might not want to finish the drink once you've done the trick, so it would be best to advise them of that fact before you start in order to avoid a smack in the mouth.

Your proud boast will be that you can fish an ice cube from the drink using a thread but without touching the drink, the ice cube or the glass.

Using a glass of water and an ice cube from the bar will sidestep any danger of the aforementioned smack in the mouth.

All you have to do is this . . .

1

Lean across to the table next door where they're having fish and chips and borrow their salt. Lay the thread across the ice cube and sprinkle on a little salt. This is what would make the drink undrinkable – unless, perhaps, it's a margarita.

2 The salt will melt the surface of the ice cube, which should then refreeze, trapping the thread. Wait a few seconds to make sure that the ice has refrozen.

TIP:
If you want to be really impressive you could pull out one of your hairs and lift the cube with that. If you can't stand the pain, then there should be a hair somewhere in your pub food.

3 You can now gently fish the ice cube out of the drink.

If only they'd had a mountain of salt and a giant rope on the Titanic . . .

Fiver Live

This is an excellent way to dodge buying a round. Bet your friend that you can set fire to his fiver and then buy you both a drink with it.

You'll need a box of matches, naturally, and a glass of brandy. The technique is very simple.

1 Soak the fiver in brandy.

2 Make sure you get plenty of brandy on the fiver.

3 Then you just set light to it. The brandy will burn off, leaving the fiver unscathed, if a little soggy.

WARNING:
Make sure you use plenty of brandy and make sure you blow out the flame before all the brandy has burned off, otherwise the fiver will go up in smoke! Also, don't get too much on your hands otherwise the keen little flame will travel up your arm. Mind you, your friends will find it very funny.

The Key

Quick! Order up another lager. For this trick you will, yet again, need a full pint and six keys of the mortise-lock type — you know, an eye at one end and the toothy bit and prong at the other. The keys must all be roughly the same size.

The challenge on which you are going to win a fortune is: How do you suspend the full pint of lager six inches above the table using only the six keys?

Impossible? Can't be done? Look and learn, suckers!

1 The key to this trick (and if stupid puns have no place in this book, where on earth are they supposed to live?) is to link the keys together like a weird free-form Meccano set. Start with two keys. Slip one through the eye of the other and stand them on the table with the teeth acting as 'feet'.

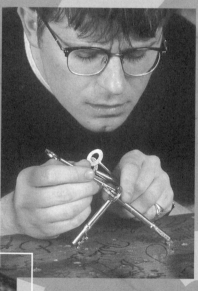

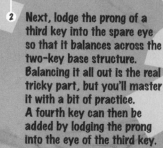

2 Next, lodge the prong of a third key into the spare eye so that it balances across the two-key base structure. Balancing it all out is the real tricky part, but you'll master it with a bit of practice. A fourth key can then be added by lodging the prong into the eye of the third key.

3 You will now see a zig-zag effect in your miniature scaffolding of keys. Place the fifth key's prong into the fourth key's eye.

TIP:
You will need to find the right kind of keys for this trick and practise a lot in order to perfect the scaffolding technique. It's worth the effort, though, as the end result is so impressive (well, it is to small children and drunks. Or small drunk children).

4 The fifth key should have a large eye so that the final key lies flat. It should now be possible to balance the full pint on top of the sixth key.

5 You now have yet another work of art better than any in a gallery due to the fact that you can drink part of this one!

Strike a

The question is, how do you light this ordinary household light bulb without plugging it in?

What you need is a glass half-filled with water, and a microwave oven.

OK, so you might need a very understanding landlord to do this one in the pub, unless you bring your own light bulb and microwave with you, but they're hardly ideal accessories to take on a night out.

All you have to do is . . .

Light

1. Stand the light bulb in the glass of water so the bulb is sticking out the top and put it in the microwave.

2. Shut the door and switch on the microwave as though you're heating up a cup of tea.

3. The light bulb will start to glow.

The bulb might well burn out quite quickly and it's not a good idea to leave it cooking for more than a few seconds, anyway.

Blow Me

You'll need a pint for this trick – it won't come to any harm, so you can use your own – and a burning match.

What you have to do is extinguish the flame without waving it around, stubbing it out, snuffing it out with your fingers or using your hands in any way, dipping it in the beer or blowing on the match.

The way to do it is simple:

NOTE: This trick was first performed in the Royal Box at Wembley Stadium on *TFI Friday* in honour of the next day's Chelsea–Middlesbrough Cup Final. My match was better.

1 Hold the lit match on the opposite side of the pint glass.

2
Crouch down and blow on the glass. Your breath will go round the glass and the flame will go out without you having blown on the match.

You might like to introduce this trick by saying that you can breath through beer, but that's even more of a cheat.

Which Can

This challenge, based on some eerie laws of carbohydrate science, can be posed in a number of ways, but the basic question is: how do you take two cans of similar-tasting fizzy drink, and make one of them float and the other sink?

All you need for this trick is a fish tank. 'A fish tank?' I hear you ask. 'Where am I going to find one of them down my local?' Well, you don't have to use a fish tank for this trick – you can use a large basin full of water, a sink, or even a deep puddle outside the pub. The fish tank just makes this trick easier to photograph.

Here's how it's done.

1 The trick is to take two cans of drink of the same brand – but make sure one of them is the diet version.

2 All you then do is lower them into your tank or basin full of water.

Can?

③ Amazingly, the diet drink will float whilst the regular one, including all those tasty additives, will sink. So watch out what you drink the next time you go swimming.

CAUTION:
You can turn this into a game of Russian Roulette by already having the two cans and the tank and asking friends to bet on which will float and which will sink, or whether both will sink. However, given that there aren't many options, maybe it's best not to bet your house and its contents on this one.

Coining it

This is a much safer bet than the last trick. Nobody will believe that you can get fifty five-pence coins into a full glass of water without touching the glass and without removing any of the water – without, in fact, spilling a drop!

Can't be done? Of course it can! All you need is fifty 5ps from the bank (why do I always queue behind you?) and a glass.

1. Fill a glass to the brim with water, and start slowly dropping 5ps into it. To avoid disturbing the surface of the water you must slip the coins in very carefully at the rim of the glass, one by one, allowing them to slide down the side into the bottom. Don't worry, surface tension is on your side.

2 Work your way around the glass to achieve an even distribution of coins. You will see the surface of the water start to bulge impossibly above the rim of the glass, but it won't spill as long as you are extremely gentle.

3 Impossible but true – fifty five-pence coins in an ordinary glass of water!

NOTE: This one you can really draw out. If you start by filling the glass and then offering bets on how many 5ps you can fit in without spilling a drop you can spin it out for ages and soon have the whole pub watching.

Eggsact Science

How do you get an ordinary hardboiled egg (best make sure it's hardboiled before you try to peel off the shell!) into a milk bottle without bursting the egg?

Can't be done? Drum roll please ...

1 What you have to do is light a piece of paper and drop it into the bottle.

2 With the paper well alight, but before it has burned away too far, place the egg on top of the bottle. It will help if you moisten the outside of the egg with a little water.

3 The egg will seal the mouth of the bottle and the burning paper will go out once it has used up all of the air inside the bottle.

This creates a vacuum which will then start to pull the egg gently into the bottle.

CAUTION:
Make sure you use a smallish egg. If you use a giant egg – one that the hen strained over for a fortnight – it might well explode rather than being sucked into the bottle and your mates aren't going to appreciate being splattered with eggy shrapnel!

4 The egg will elongate as it is sucked in and the moistened surface will help it to slide down the neck of the bottle.

5 Hey presto! The egg lands in the bottom of the bottle and bounces back into shape!

The Banana

Following on from the Eggsact Science egg-in-a-bottle trick, this is a similar stunt with a banana.

Your mission, Jim, should you choose to accept it, is to remove the inside of the banana whole, without peeling it and using only a milk bottle. Squeezing, slicing, cutting, pushing or any form of violence are not allowed. The end of the banana, however, must already be open.

The technique is the same as for the egg trick.

1 Drop a lighted piece of paper into the bottle.

Splits

2

Place the open end of the banana over the neck of the bottle with the flaps of the banana skin on the outside.

3

This will form a seal, just as the egg did before, and the inside of the banana will now be sucked out of the skin and into the bottle.

How you get the banana out of the bottle is your own business.

Water into

Here's a stunt of biblical proportions – turning water into wine!

Before your very eyes you will see a full glass of water swap places with a full glass of red wine. You don't have to empty them out, you don't have to syphon them off and you can do it without spilling a drop, using only a piece of thick paper.

How do you perform such a miracle? Read on...

1. Cover the top of the glass of water with the piece of thick paper, pressing down firmly with the palm of your hand.

2. Turn the glass upside down, maintaining the pressure on the paper.

Wine

3 If the paper is tight to the glass, you should now be able to take your hand away and the paper will prevent this turning into that other bible story about the Great Flood.

4 Now place the glass of water on top of the glass full of red wine, rim to rim with the paper sandwiched in between. You now have to gently pull the paper out a fraction from between the glasses.

5 Pull the paper out a little more until you have a gap no more than a quarter of the way across the surface of the glass.

6 It will take a few minutes to transfer completely, but the water will slowly sep down to take the place of the wine, with the wine climbing up into the water glass.

Hallelujah!

Queen of

You can bet a tenner on this, if you're brave enough. Your boast is that you can take your mate's tenner and turn the Queen into the Queen of Australia* – ie turn her upside down, without turning the tenner over.

Learn these moves carefully – it could cost you a tenner if you don't!

1

Fold the tenner in half longways by turning the top edge down towards you.

* If you're reading in Australia, yes I know you're independent of HerMajesty, but just go along with it for heaven's sake

x

Australia

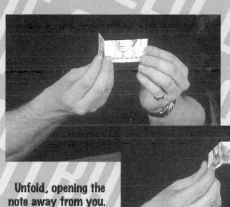

Fold it in half again, bringing the right-hand side behind the left. **2**

Unfold, opening the note away from you. **3**

4 Unfold longways, again opening the note away from you.

The Queen is now upside down and you're a tenner better off!

Table

This is a feat of strength that will astound your local saloon bar and win you such respect that you will probably be bought drinks on the house for the rest of your life. Pass this secret on to your first-born child and your family may never have to buy a drink for generations. Centuries ago, it helped my family escape slavery from the Romans, and, who knows? in the future could bring about world peace.

Anyway, the challenge to throw out to the assembled throng is, how do you lift an ordinary small bar table _from above_ using only a beer glass, a beer mat and a match? Remember, you are lifting from above, with no support underneath the table.

Can't be done? It blimmin' well can. Let others try it first.

1 First of all, make sure the beer mat is sopping wet and slap it down in the middle of the table. Then, stand your match upright on the beer mat, sticking it in to the suface of the mat to do so.

Set fire to the match head before . . . **2**

Dancer

3 Cramming the pint glass down on to the beer mat, pushing it down as hard as you can to create an air-tight seal between the mat and the glass. Make sure you don't put the match out as you do this. The match has to burn long enough to use up all the air.

WARNING:
Make sure that you lift the glass straight up. If you tilt it at all you could ruin the seal, destroying the vacuum. You will, however, still be lifting hard and you are liable to smack yourself in the nose with the bottom of the glass.

4 Once the match goes out, you should have created a strong enough vacuum inside the glass to allow you to lift the table off the floor. Enjoy the moment.

Match of

This is a perplexing little conundrum. You have two upturned pint glasses (empty ones, dummy), a match balanced delicately between them and a matchbox underneath one of them.

How do you get the matchbox out from under the pint glass without disturbing the match suspended between the two?

Can't be done? Wanna bet? All you have to do is . . .

1 Set fire to the head of the suspended match, allowing it to flare up before gently blowing it out.

the Day

2 Leave it a few seconds to settle and the match will have welded itself to the glass and you can remove the other glass, leaving the match in place.

3 You are now free to pick up the matchbox. Ta-da!

Holding Folding

For this trick you will need a ten-pound note – someone else's if you plan to win it in a bet and you can find someone gullible enough – and three wine glasses.

The bet is that you can stand a wine glass on the ten-pound note suspended between the other two glasses. It doesn't look very likely. Most crumpled old tenners, in fact, hardly look capable of supporting themselves between two glasses, let alone bear the weight of a glass, but it can be done.

1 Make a series of folds longways on the tenner, creating a tight, corrugated effect. About six folds should be sufficient.

2 The corrugated note should now make a perfect bridge between the two glasses and be perfectly capable of . . .

3 . . . taking the weight of the third glass.

A Pinch

A plastic comb is something you might carry with you on a night out, but salt and pepper aren't, so you'll have to make sure you're in a pub that serves food, otherwise this trick is a bit of a non-starter.

What you have to do is pour a little salt on to the table (make sure the table is nice and dry with no puddles of spilt lager slopping around) then sprinkle some pepper on to the salt and mix it up with your finger.

The question is, how do you separate the pepper from the salt without touching or disturbing the salt and using only your trusty (and clean and fairly new) back-pocket comb?

Can't be done? It can with a full head of hair.

# of Salt

1 Run the comb through your hair a few times.

2 Pass the comb slowly over your salt and pepper mix. Keep it close to the surface, but don't touch the salt. Watch carefully and you will see the pepper jumping up on to the statically charged comb.

3 Tap the comb on to your hand and the pepper will drop out.

You now have a handful of pepper, skilfully separated from the mound of salt. Now if you only had some egg, chips and beans to go with it. Where is that menu?

All Fingers

This is an exercise in manual dexterity which, with a little bit of practice, could win you a drink or two.

What you need is a wine glass and two coins. The coins, 20p pieces in this case, need to be balanced opposite each other on the rim of the glass.

Now you can bet your mates that you can remove the coins from the glass at the same time, using only your thumb and forefinger of one hand and without dropping them on the table or picking up the glass.

Here's how:

1 Place your thumb and forefinger on the coins and gently tip them over the edge of the glass together.

2 The coins will be trapped between your fingers and the glass. You can carefully slide them down around the bowl of the glass.

& Thumbs

3 Keep the coins going down on to the stem of the glass and then pause.

4 Finally, pinch the coins off the stem in one swift action. You now have 40p and a smug grin.

Got the Bottle

For this trick you will need a match, a 5p coin and an empty wine bottle. (OK, it doesn't have to be a wine bottle or, indeed, empty, but empty wine bottles are all I seem to have in my house.)

Fold the match so that it forms a right angle, then place it on top of the open bottle. Next balance the coin on top of the match.

Now, how do you get the coin into the bottle without touching the match, the bottle or the coin? Just for a change, you're not allowed to blow on it or burn it, either!

1 Dribble a little water, or beer, on to the match.

2 Watch as the match slowly straightens out.

3 The coin will then drop into the bottom of the bottle.

Cool Cube

How do you set fire to a sugar cube?

Sounds easy, doesn't it? But if you just put a match to it, the cube won't burn. No, you can't go and syphon some petrol out of the landlord's Jag. The answer lies on the very table at which you are sitting supping your pint.

1 Simply dip the corner of the sugar cube in the nearest ashtray.

2 You only need a tiny spot of ash on the cube.

3 Then, hold a lighted match up to the ash spot.

4 The cube will now start to burn.

CAUTION:
Remember to blow out the sugar before the flames reach your fingers – unless you want a caramelised hand.

Give it a

This one will intrigue any of your mates who are secret brandy drinkers and want to know how they can get at that Christmas bottle in the cupboard without anyone knowing they've been in there. The bet is, you see, that you can drink a measure of brandy from an unopened bottle. The secret boozer will take you up on it just to find out how!

Here's how you con them out of a pint!

1) Take a measure of brandy, either from the bar or use someone else's drink – best ask first!

Shot

2 Tip the unopened brandy bottle upside down and pour the measure of brandy into the recess in the bottom of the bottle.

3 Drink it. You're drinking from an unopened bottle! Oh, come on! Whaddya mean it's a con? You've just won a pint!

Mine's a

Actually, this trick is really a treble - three challenges in one. First, how do you put two full pints of water (no point in wasting beer on this trick) mouth to mouth without spilling any? Secondly, how do you drop a coin into the two-pint stack without spilling the water; and finally, how do you empty out one of the glasses without touching either glass?

All you'll need is a tank of water or a large basin - you know, the one from Which Can Can?

①
First, you submerge the two glasses in the basin of water and, once they're full and all of the air bubbles have stopped, hold them tight together, rim to rim.

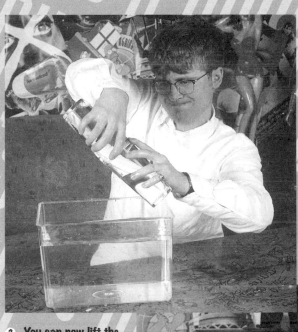

Double

2 You can now lift the glasses out of the water, keeping them tight together so that there are no spills or leakages.

3 The first part of the trick is now accomplished – one pint is stacked on top of another. So, how do you get the coin in there?

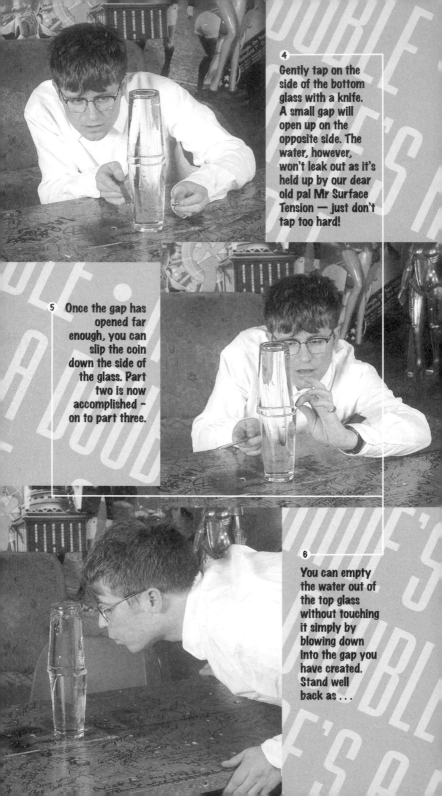

4 Gently tap on the side of the bottom glass with a knife. A small gap will open up on the opposite side. The water, however, won't leak out as it's held up by our dear old pal Mr Surface Tension — just don't tap too hard!

5 Once the gap has opened far enough, you can slip the coin down the side of the glass. Part two is now accomplished – on to part three.

6 You can empty the water out of the top glass without touching it simply by blowing down into the gap you have created. Stand well back as . . .

7 . . .the water will quickly flood out all over the table.

8 You are then left with an empty top glass and a bit of a mess on the table – sorry! Hopefully, you'll have read this bit before you started the trick!

Low-Gravity

Can you make ordinary lager defy gravity?

Yet another pint (haven't you had enough, sir?) is required for this spectacular stunt. What you are going to do is hold the pint upside down above your head without the contents pouring out and soaking you, and without using any other props.

It might be best to use somebody else's pint for a couple of good reasons:

a) If it goes wrong you won't have wasted your own beer and they won't mind because they'll be too busy laughing at you.

b) You will tell everyone beforehand that if you can do it you will keep the pint.

The technique is as follows:

❶

Hold the pint with your thumb pointing away from you and fingers curled round towards you. Like a forehand shot, for those of you who play tennis.

WARNING:
This trick is extra tricky, i.e. impossible, in one of those quaint old pubs with low beams. Mind you, if you drink in one of those pubs, you've probably already been thrown out.

Beer

2 Keeping your elbow perfectly straight, rotate your arm like a windmill. You have to do this quite fast.

3 At the top of the swing, the pint will be upside down above your head, but the lager will stay in the glass – as long as you keep moving. At this point you will also have to twist your wrist round.

4 The twist of the wrist means that you end up at the bottom of the swing in a 'backhand' position with your fingers away from your body. Twisting your wrist is a good idea because it stops your shoulder from dislocating.

You have now either won yourself another pint or ruined your best shirt. Get your friends to try it now.

Burn in

Brave, unflinching and hard as nails, you will impress everyone when you hold a burning cigarette between thumb and forefinger without so much as a whimper.

Lay it down as a challenge, put money on it, wager drinks. You can do it, but no one else around the table will be able to.

How's it done? You need a very special secret weapon – an ice cube.

① While casually talking to your friends, taking bets or whatever, you will be holding one hand just below the table. Between your thumb and forefinger you will have an ice cube.

Hell

2 Hold the ice cube for several minutes, until your finger has gone numb.

3 With your cold and numbed finger, from which you have wiped the wetness on your trousers, you will now be able to hold the burning end.

TIP:
There's no point trying this challenge in the Sado-Masochists' Arms.

Cuff Him

Never play this trick on a friend you want to keep. What you are going to do is hold up two pints and bet him a fiver that he can't drink them both once you have put them down. He will be able to touch both pint glasses, but you will bet him that he can't finish the pints, drinking first from one and then the other.

It's a difficult bet for your friend to resist, especially if you have just got the beers in. Get him to slap his fiver down on the table.

That fiver is as good as yours, and here's how you win it . . .

1   Get your friend to place his hands flat on the table, palms down.

2   Make as if to hand him the pints but, instead, balance a pint on the back of each of his hands.

With a pint on the back of each hand, your friend cannot move. If he does he will spill two pints of beer over himself.

3

4 Take the fiver and leave him there. In fact, take his wallet out of his jacket and buy a round for everyone in the bar. Your friend won't be able to stop you and it serves him right for being greedy in the first place.

Follow My

Here's another trick you can play on a friend – or, if you've run out, maybe it's time to introduce yourself to that old man who's sat and mumbled to himself on that bar stool for the last three years.

All you need is two half-pints, two boxes of matches and your gullible stooge. Once you get the gist of this trick, you will see that it can easily be adapted to include other props and drinks.

Bet your friend a drink that he can't follow your actions exactly, one step at a time, using his left hand when you use yours, his right when you use yours, drinking from his glass when you drink from yours, etc. Then embark on the following bizarre routine, remaining silent and concentrated throughout.

Leader?

1 Take a sip from your half-pint, using your right hand. Replace the glass exactly where it was.

2 Your friend does likewise.

3 Take two matches out of the box and lay them parallel on the table. Replace the box exactly where it was.

4 Your friend does likewise.

5 Take two more matches from the box and form them into a square. Replace the box exactly where it was.

6 Your friend does likewise.

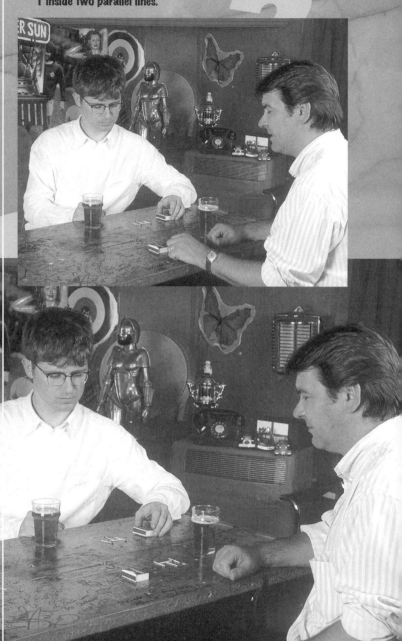

8 Your friend does likewise.

9 Take another sip of beer using your right hand. Replace the glass exactly where it was.

10 Your friend does likewise.

11 Take one match from your pattern and put it back in the box. Replace the box exactly where it was.

Your friend does likewise. **12**

⑬ **Pick up your glass and spit a huge mouthful of beer back into it. You didn't swallow your second mouthful.**

⑭ **Your friend is pole-axed. Gutted. Lonely as a bastard on Father's Day.**

If you don't win a drink doing this, you never will.

TIP:
Obviously you have to make a great show of being very precise about everything in order to hoodwink your friend into following what you are doing and distract him from noticing that you haven't swallowed your beer. You must also insist beforehand on complete silence, otherwise you can't hold the beer in your mouth while you go through all of the actions.

Raise a

Bottles are fairly heavy things, even when they are empty, and drinking straws are quite puny little things. So how do you lift an ordinary (empty) wine bottle off the table using only an ordinary drinking straw and without tying any knots in the straw?

The problem may appear to defy the laws of nature, but, after 4.5 billion years of evolution*, we have learnt how to do pub tricks like this.

1. The first step is to bend the straw a few centimetres from the bottom. Straws being what they are, it will try to spring back straight again. That's good: that springiness is just what you want.

Bottle

Next you insert the folded end of the straw into the neck of the bottle. Push it down slowly until it reaches the part where the bottle starts to widen. The straw will now try to spring open.

3 Gently ease the straw down into the bottle until, when you try to pull it back, the opening straw jams against the bottom of the bottle neck, allowing you to lift the entire bottle off the table.

*I knew that degree in zoology would come in handy one day.

Leaning Pint

Here we go, defying the laws of nature again. Well, almost. This trick really is a bit of a con, but it looks great when you leave a pint sitting on a table leaning like the Tower of Pisa. Set it up while your friend is in the gentlemen's/ladies' and, when he or she returns, they will wonder if they've maybe had one too many.

But just how do you make an almost full pint lean over using only a beer mat and a matchstick?

1   Put the matchstick tight against the edge of the beer mat.

# of Pisa

Tilt your pint slightly and slide the beer mat in underneath. 2

You then remove the beer mat, leaving the matchstick behind and the pint leaning like the Tower of Pisa with no visible means of support. 3

It's a Jaffa

We've all seen smarmy magicians on telly making a silver sphere or crystal ball dance along the edge of a swathe of silk. You can do the same with an orange and a tea towel in the pub.

Just take an ordinary tea towel or napkin, let everyone see it, even ask someone to pass it to you in the first place. Next you need an orange. Again, you can ask someone to pass this to you. Holding a corner of the napkin in one hand, you carefully place the orange underneath. The fun is about to begin.

1 Hold up the napkin and look as though you are concentrating very hard on something.

2 Slowly the orange will start to appear.

3 To cries of wonder and amazement the orange will slowly rise up and start dancing and bobbing at the edge of the napkin.

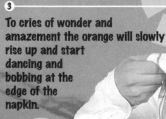

Fake

How on earth did you manage to perform such an incredible feat – especially after all you've had to drink? Easy – you cheated!

1. Either beforehand or when you're secreting the orange under the napkin, you jam it on the end of a fork which you have hidden under the napkin. Make sure you stick the fork in near the bottom of the orange.

2. When you hold up the napkin, you have the orange speared on the fork, which remains hidden behind the napkin, and you can bounce the orange around as much as you like as long as you keep the fork out of sight.

This is a good trick to do out of nowhere, without any set-up. Then people will have no idea what you're doing.

Ashes to

This is a bit of magic that never fails to impress, especially if your friend has had a couple of drinks. You will tell your friend that you can scientifically prove whether he or she is, or ever will be, a smoker.

The preparation for this trick is vital, and must be done in secret without your stooge seeing.

1. Rub your right index finger in an ashtray, picking up a deposit of ash. Do this while your friend is in the loo or at the bar.

Ashes

2 Once your stooge is present, ask him to stretch his hands out staight in front of him. Demonstrate this yourself, palms down of course. This will make him believe that you have nothing in you hands.

3 When he stretches out his hands, grab hold of them as if you are straightening them properly, telling him that he must hold them perfectly steady. As you do this, rub the ash from your fingertip into the palm of his hand without him noticing.

4 Next you ask him to clench his fists tight and start giving him an intense spiel about how he should now be focusing his feelings and spirits towards his clenched fist.

5 You then make a great show of sprinkling a little ash on the back of his hand, or both his hands if you have 'infected' both of his palms.

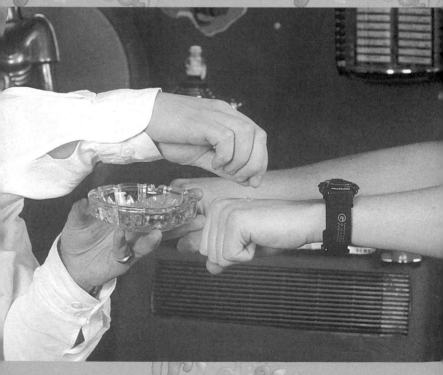

6 Explain to him that, if he is really a smoker deep down, the ash on the back of his hand will have absorbed into his bloodstream and now it is travelling through his body. In a second he will be sweating it out through his closed palm. Make the most of this speech and tell him to concentrate hard.

7 Make a big thing of the concentration and tell him to open his fist after a count of five. The ash has travelled through his closed fist.

Gracefully accept the adulation, applause and offers of free drinks.

Sole Man

This is another great trick to freak people out, especially when their minds have been slightly loosened by booze. Once you've learnt how to do it you can 'dress it up' with whatever ridiculous words you want.

Tell your victim you know what sort of personality he has and can prove it to him using a deck of cards.

This trick is all about 'leading' your victim to a card of choice.

1 First, before you set up the challenge put somewhere about your person a card of your choice. For example, I've stuck the jack of diamonds to my shoe.

2 Ask your victim to choose a suit colour – red or black. If he chooses red, then say, 'OK that suggests you are warm and compassionate.' If he chooses black say, 'So that leaves you with red, which means you are warm and compassionate.'

3 Ask him to choose the red suit (heart or diamonds) that describe him best. If he chooses diamonds say something like, 'Diamonds – yes, you are bright and shiny, yet hard.' If he chooses hearts say, 'So that leaves you with diamonds. So you are bright and shiny, yet hard.'

Continue leading him to the card by giving him a choice of royal/non royal, then jack and queen/king and ace, then jack/queen. After each selection equate his choice with his 'personality' as before. He has now 'chosen' the jack of diamonds.

4

5 Finally, with a flourish, lift your leg and throw it on to the table revealing that card stuck to your shoe. You always knew he was the jack of diamonds!

NOTE: This is even cleverer if you can somehow place the card about his person, although it may be tricky if he catches you with your hand in his back pocket.

Breast Left

You either need to be very brave to carry out this bet, or have a female friend with a great sense of humour – and Lord knows those can be hard enough to find. (Only joking, ladies, please!)

What you are going to do is bet your extremely good-humoured lady friend £1 that you can make her boobs move up and down without touching her boobs or any other part of her body.

①
You may need to make up some highly convincing codswallop about gravity, the moon, magnetism or psychokinesis to hoodwink your friend. The psychokinesis one is pretty good. You can bumble on for ages about controlled experiments in Russia involving moving objects on tables, muscle manipulation and levitation, etc.

Unsaid

2 Unless you are some kind of Uri Geller with added mammary mind power, you won't be able to make your freind's breasts move at all and, what's more, you never intended to, you lowlife. Gently grasp the lady's brasts and move them up and down.

WARNING:
Some women may never speak to you again if you pull this stunt on them. Some blokes will go crazy if you con them out of a pint. Given the effect a fist can have on the delicate bones in the nose, this is definitely a bad thing.

3 Then coolly hand over the £1. You've lost the bet but the experience was probably worth a quid!

This trick also works with a mate's pint. Bet him 50p you can make it disappear without touching it, then pick it up and down it in one. 50p for a pint is a bargain!

The Grey

This one, amazingly, works nearly every time. Just don't try it too late at night – maths in the head isn't too easy. You are going to read the mind of one or, more impressively, several of your friends. Like this:

1 Ask them to pick a number between one and ten – tell them not to say it out loud.

2 Then ask them to add five to it.

Elephant

3 Then get them to double the number they have.

4 Tell them to subtract two.

6 Next they halve it.

7 Then they take away the number they first thought of from the current total.

7   Tell them to imagine the alphabet as numbers – so A = 1, B = 2, etc – and now to assign a letter to the number they have.

8   Now ask them to think of a country beginning with that letter and remember it.

9   Now tell them to move to the next letter of the alphabet, and think of an animal beginning with that letter, and a colour they'd associate with that animal.

10 Grandly announce to all and sundry that they are now thinking of a grey elephant from Denmark. You'll be right.

TIP:
Be careful about trying this with a zoologist or geography student otherwise you may end up with a magenta echidna from Djibouti. (And if anyone's bad at maths expect a brown warthog from Venezuela.)

I've Got Piles

For this challenge you will need a selection of coins.

First of all, you'll need nine 2p pieces stacked up in a column on the table.

Then you'll need a 50p, a 2p, a 10p, a £1, a 20p, a 1p and a 5p, and any other coins that have been minted since we did this.

① Lay the other coins out in a line, stretching away from the stack in order of size.

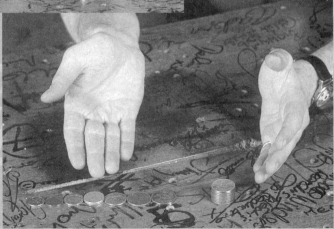

2 Now challenge, or better still bet, everyone to guess which of the coins, when standing on edge, will match the height of the column of 2p pieces.

3 Everyone will guess differently. The 50p looks favourite as it's biggest and the 2p also look likely. Give them one chance to pick up a coin and put it on end alongside the stack. They'll be wrong and lose the bet. You then pick up the 5p, the smallest coin of all.

4 The 5p is the one that exactly matches the height of the stack.

Up in

How do you clear the smoke from a bottle full of smoke? This is a good trick to do as a follow up to Eggsact Science or The Banana Splits, but, if you haven't performed one of these incredible tricks, then you must do as follows:

1. Light a piece of paper and drop it in your bottle.

2 Let it burn itself out and you will have a bottle full of smoke.

Smoke

So, how do you clear the smoke?
Don't even think about sucking it out with a
straw – that really wouldn't be good for you.

3 Pour some brandy into the bottle. You don't
need too much. Take an ordinary measure of
brandy, pour in about half and drink the rest.
See – I told you there would be some reward
to sticking with this book.

4 Next, strike a match and drop it into the bottle. Be careful when you do this as there is a chance that the brandy might flare up. You don't want to lose your eyebrows. (This is the pub trick Michael Jackson was performing the the mid-80s when he set fire to his hair. Sorry, Michael.)

5 The brandy will burn off, clearing the smoke from the bottle as it does so.

6 You are then left with a totally clear bottle and, even if you do this trick in a conference of inorganic chemists, an audience scratching their heads.

Step Into

How do you climb through an ordinary Christmas card, or birthday card as used in our little demonstration, and step into Christmas? (Step Into Birthday doesn't have quite the same ring to it, does it?) Pluck a card from the pub wall and challenge your disbelieving friends.

It may seem unlikely that a hulking great brute of a bloke (for the purposes of these photographs, it's a sulking great fruit of a bloke) can pass his entire body through this card, but it can be done. Here's how:

Christmas

1 Cut a slit in the card running parallel with the bottom going from the folded edge towards the open edge. Do not cut all the way to the open edge. Leave a space a little bigger that the strip your have just created.

2 Turn the card round and cut a second strip from the open edge towards the fold. Again, do not cut all the way. Repeat steps 1. and 2. all the way up the card, creating a series of evenly spaced slashes. You must finish with a cut going from the spine towards the open edge.

3 Next, snip through all of the folded 'spine' ends of your strips except for the one at the top and the one at the bottom of the card.

4

You can now open out the whole card into a huge loop of paper.

5 Treat the fragile loop gently.
It will open up quite wide,
hopefully wide enough for
you to climb through.
Merry Christmas, everybody!
The drinks are on me!

**Congratulations.
You are now a Pub Genius.**

Now, how about a conversation?